TO CARIBOO AND BACK IN 1862

Of this edition _______copies were finished and bound.

This is Copy No._______.

TO
CARIBOO
AND BACK IN 1862

W. CHAMPNESS

YE GALLEON PRESS

Fairfield, Washington

1972

Library of Congress Cataloging in Publication Data

Champness, W
   To Cariboo and back in 1862.

   Originally published serially in the Leisure hour, April 1865, under the title: To Cariboo and back.
   1. Cariboo District. 2. British Columbia – Description and travel. 3. Champness, W. I. Title.
F1089.C3C52   1972   917.11'04'2   73-22291
ISBN 0-87770-109-1

ISBN 0-87770-109-1

GORDON BOWES, 1913-1971

INTRODUCTION

OLD WAS DISCOVERED on the creeks of the Cariboo in 1860 and in 1861; and when the news reached beyond British Columbia, a second major influx of prospectors and speculators began in 1862. But, unlike the first rush to the Fraser River in 1858, there were fewer Americans and more Britons in the Cariboo rush, due partially to the reports which Donald Fraser submitted to the London *Times*. In the spring of 1862, an observant Englishman named W. Champness set out with his nephew for the Cariboo. He had "seen the elephant", but he did not find the wealth he sought. In fact, he found only experience, hardship, and mosquitoes, but the account of his great adventure which appeared serially in England in *The Leisure Hour: A Family Journal of Instruction and Recreation* (April 1, 8, 15, 22, and 29, 1865) captures the vigor and courage of the unsuccessful and disillusioned argonaut. Unfortunately, we know nothing about Champness, but he seems to have remained in Victoria following his return from the mines in December

INTRODUCTION

1862, at least he was still there in 1865. The narrative, which was edited with additions from rough notes and sketches which Champness had sent from Victoria, is little known and seldom read today; and although relatively brief, the literate and descriptive account of Champness' experiences, observations, and disappointments provides an insight into the mining frontier of British Columbia a century and more ago.

Champness travelled by sea to Aspinwall, across Panama by rail, thence to San Francisco on one of Commodore Vanderbilt's overcrowded and uncomfortable steamers, finally arriving in Victoria on the *Sierra Nevada,* probably in the first days of June 1862. He remained in that crowded city of haphazard buildings only a few days before setting out for the mines of Cariboo. From New Westminster he travelled the Douglas Road via Harrison Lake and thence by lake and trail to Lillooet, where the small party reprovisioned at exorbitant rates and secured horses for the overland trip to Antler Creek in the Cariboo through tangles of downed timber, soggy swamps, and over precipice-clinging trails. Dispirited by the arduous labours of the trip, the high cost of supplies, and the difficulty of locating gold, Champness remained at the mines only two weeks before turning back in mid-July. To recoup his rapidly dwindling resources, he worked for three months at a large farm in the valley of the Thompson River, and with the onset of winter he returned to Victoria. Champness' account gives

INTRODUCTION

to the modern reader a graphic picture of the rigours of the route followed by the miners into Cariboo, particularly before improvements on the Douglas Road and the completion of the Great North Road (Cariboo Road) up the Fraser and Thompson Rivers from Yale to Clinton made travel by wagon and stage possible in 1863. And the narrative of the rugged life (for both man and beast) along the trail with the monotonous fare of beans and bacon and sometimes only tea, serves to remind us of the dispiriting hardships encountered by the early-day miners. Descriptions of the Indians and their customs, particularly in the vicinity of Lytton, further enhance this account. The trip was not without its moments of wonderment and humour, however, and today's reader can well understand Champness' amazed reaction at coming upon a pack train of camels lumbering clumsily through a swampy morass, or his joy at being able to indulge in "a good wash, the only really cheap comfort obtainable in British Columbia." Despite his praise for the blessings of the security and stability of British law in British Columbia, particularly when compared with the "flagrant and atrocious" happenings in California, the reader is left with the strong feeling that Champness really did not care for the farthest reaches of Empire where flour cost twenty-five cents and more a pound and where an income of £250 was necessary to secure the comforts which in England were to be had for £100.

INTRODUCTION

Champness leaves the reader intrigued. Why, for instance, having toiled and strained to reach the Cariboo, did he devote so little of his account to a description of life and conditions in that area. He went no farther than Antler Creek, yet just across Bold Mountain that very summer Billy Barker was prospecting on Williams Creek where gold had been discovered the previous year. On August 13, 1862, Barker entered a claim on which the gold that resulted in the rush to Barkerville was discovered about 21 August, only four weeks after Champness had begun his return trip. Some 5,000 miners travelled to Cariboo during 1862, and an estimated $2,656,903 in gold was taken from the sands and gravels of its creeks that year. Thus, its prospects were far from being as gloomy as Champness portrayed them. Yet, distance and cost were always to be major factors in the Cariboo diggings, and it is in his descriptions of the rugged British Columbia terrain, the comments on the difficulties and discouragements of travel and transport, life on the trail or in the road houses where adulterated whisky and unrestrained gambling were threats to both health and pocketbook, and the beginnings of agricultural development in the interior that make the re-publication of this neglected account of one frustrated miner's experiences a welcome addition to the relatively small number of published narratives by participants in the opening of Cariboo.

INTRODUCTION

The late Gordon Bowes of Vancouver, who was for many years a prominent member of the British Columbia Historical Association, hoped that Champness' "To Cariboo and Back" would someday be reprinted, and prior to his tragic death in an auto accident in the summer of 1971 he had initiated such a project. It is very fitting, then, that in memory of Mr. Bowes this delightful series of articles is once again made available through the joint efforts of Ye Galleon Press and the British Columbia Historical Association.

William R. Sampson,
University of Alberta,
17 August, 1972.

HIS VOLUME IS AN effort on the part of the British Columbia Historical Association to finalize a work that a truly dedicated British Columbian had been attempting to accomplish for some time before his untimely death in 1971.

Gordon Bowes loved books with a kind of reverence that is not common to many people. He had a great love for his Province, and in particular, the history of the people who have shaped its destiny. He sincerely believed that the recorded history of British Columbia should be made available to everyone, and that noteworthy items long out of print should be reprinted in such a way as to retain as much of the feeling of the time as would be possible to place within two covers. He had found this narrative by W. Champness and had spent a considerable amount of time, without success, endeavouring to discover who this man was who had written such an exciting account of his adventures and who had the added ability to illustrate his work so delightfully. Gordon held this work in

INTRODUCTION

such high esteem that he had persuaded his friend Glen Adams of Ye Galleon Press to consider reprinting it.

Gordon was an active participant and believer in the work of local historical societies, and gave unstintingly of his time and energy to encourage their establishment. He was a leader with the happy knack of being able to establish harmony among strongly conflicting opinions, in keeping with his tolerant attitudes.

How better could the British Columbia Historical Association pay tribute to the memory of one of its most respected members than to help complete one of his unfinished projects? Although he did not realize the fulfilment of this ambition it shall be for ever to his memory that the Council and Members of the British Columbia Historical Association are proud to be able to do this for Gordon Bowes.

"The world will little note, nor long remember, what we say here, but it can never forget what they did here. It is for us, the living, rather to be dedicated here to the unfinished work they have thus far so nobly advanced."
(Abraham Lincoln - Gettysburg, 19th Nov. 1863)

Philip A. Yandle - Secretary,
British Columbia Historical
Association,
Vancouver 1972.

TTACHED TO MY GARAGE in the pleasant country village of Fairfield, Washington, there is a workshop where I print and publish books. Here I print again books and booklets many of which were first printed a hundred years or more ago, with the oldest title (and this work is still incomplete) going back to the year 1753. Here I print Oregon Trail, California Trail, Indian captivities, rare Northwest Coast, and a few such things. In a corner of the workshop there is a five drawer steel file where are kept several thousand letters, nearly all on the subject of rare western history. One thick folder is marked *Bowes, Gordon.* Here are letters discussing at length the possible printing of several items of western Canadian history, particularly Adrian Gabriel Morice, *The History of the Northern Interior of British Columbia;* and W. Champness, *To Cariboo and Back in 1862.* The Morice was managed first and I had sent an inscribed copy to Gordon. The Champness now comes along many months later. As I stood at the press hour after hour and day after

INTRODUCTION

day feeding sheets for the book I liked to feel that Gordon was in some fashion standing beside me giving me counsel and encouragement. As the thousands of printed sheets needed to make up the book slowly stacked up I could reflect on the word picture that Champness so long ago wrote of travel in and out, to and from the Cariboo gold fields. The printing was my own but the counsel, the encouragement, and the original old printed sheets had all been supplied by Gordon and to this extent we are in his debt.

I wish to thank William Sampson and Philip Yandle who furnished introductions, and Patricia Brammall who drew the pen and ink portrait of Gordon Bowes.

Serious students of British Columbia history will note that we used a simplified title in printing the Champness work.

Glen Adams
Fairfield, Washington
Late autumn, 1972

This is the gold pan, 12 to 18 inches in diameter with flared sides, used everywhere by prospectors searching for placer gold. In actual mining operations larger scale equipment would be employed.

This is the rocker or cradle, widely used in primitive placer gold mining operations. It could be constructed quickly by using a few boards whipsawed from nearby trees. Although capacity was limited it easy to operate and it required much less water than sluicing.

This is the Long Tom or sluice box, extensively used in the Cariboo and elsewhere. It was much more efficient than than the rocker.

This is the Spanish arrastra or primitive ore crushing equipment, not much used in the Cariboo but widely used elsewhere in the American West.

TO CARIBOO AND BACK IN 1862

TO CARIBOO AND BACK. AN EMIGRANT'S JOURNEY TO THE GOLD-FIELDS OF BRITISH COLUMBIA

N THE SPRING OF 1862 THE the writer accompanied by his nephew, left England for British Columbia, having resolved to emigrate to the Cariboo gold-fields, of which glowing accounts had reached us.

The first part of our journey, the three weeks' voyage from Southampton to Aspinwall, touching at St Thomas, in the West Indies, was not characterized by any particular incidents calling for special record. Inasmuch, however, as we had, for the most part, fine weather and smooth seas, it was a time of considerable interest to ourselves and to our fellow-passengers, about a hundred in number.

On landing at Aspinwall, our first impression of the Isthmus were not very agreeable; as we found the temperature there intensely hot, the skies overclouded, and a close, damp, sickly feeling pervading the atmosphere. We did not make any stay here, but at once proceeded across the Isthmus, by rail, to

Panama, a distance of forty-nine miles, which we accomplished in three hours. The scenery here passed through, and the character and construction of the railway, interested us much. The latter was originally planned and surveyed by the well-known traveller John L. Stephens, the author of "Researches amongst the Buried Cities of Central America." The line was begun in 1850, and opened throughout on January 27th, 1855. It cost six million dollars and several thousand lives. Indeed, so excessive was the mortality amongst the labourers employed in the construction, that it is a common statement hereabouts, though doubtless a very exaggerated one, that one life was sacrificed for every foot of the railway. It is also well known that, before the line was made, there was constant mortality and disease amongst the transit passengers across the Isthmus, to and from Australia, California, and the Atlantic. Even a delay of a few hours amid the hot and almost steaming morasses and jungles of the district, often produced long continuing or fatal illness. A considerable portion of the railway is over wide swamps. Here it was necessary to bury innumerable trunks of trees to form a basis for the "sleepers." In other parts the line passes through very picturesque forest scenery, but nowhere attains a height greater than two hundred and fifty feet above the ocean.

The town of Panama is prettily situated on a bay of the same name. Here we, for the first time, caught sight of the great Pacific Ocean, somewhere along the shores of which we hoped to find a second home, and, perhaps, a fortune. The houses and churches of Panama are generally in a very dilapidated condition, but, being constructed of a bright red stone,

and appearing in many cases as if almost buried in green masses of vegetation, they form a picturesque sight, especially when viewed at a little distance. But the houses of the poorer inhabitants, and those in the surrounding country, are mere log-huts of one or two rooms, and roofed with shingles or palm-leaves. The greatest ornament of the Isthmus vegetation is the coral-tree, which sometimes attains a height of sixty feet. It bears a multitude of flowers of the brightest crimson, giving a glow to the whole landscape, where there are many of these trees together. The chief products of the country hereabouts are cacao (*theobroma*), indigo, and plantains. As a rule, cacao estates are more valuable than those of sugar, indigo, cotton, or cochineal. The plantain grows most abundantly throughout Central America and the Isthmus. Green and ripe, roasted, boiled, fried, and preserved, it enters, in a hundred forms, into every meal; and, as an acre of plantains is capable of supplying nourishment equal to one hundred and thirty-three acres of wheat and moreover requires little or no attention, it follows that the country which produces it lacks one grand incentive to industry. A friend of ours noted down, after a sketch of the plantain tree in his scrapbook, "Platano, Spanish for plantain: an institution for the encouragement of laziness."

A very unmistakable proof of the indolence of the population hereabouts is furnished by their gross inattention to the simplest sanitary measures. The dead bodies of their numerous mules are allowed to decay in the most offensive proximity to human dwellings and throughfares. The evil would be absolutely intolerable but for the multitude of ravens which hover round and gratify the pecular taste which nature has given them with horrible meals of carrion.

The town of Panama is principally inhabited by a Spanish population; but there are also many Yankees, and a few Europeans. The commerce is increasing rapidly, and must continue to do so, from the peculiar position of the place, on the main connecting link between east and west, north and south. Three or four regular lines of steamers depart from and arrive at this port: the British mail line of South American steamers to Peru and Chili, and the Australian, New Zealand, and Californian lines. By the latter we had arranged to take our departure for San Francisco.

Although the population of Panama is chiefly Catholic, and the constant ringing of their bells keeps one in mind of the fact, yet there are more than a few Protestants, especially

THE GOLDEN GATE

amongst the American merchants. We were informed by a missionary that there are here thirty of forty such families, of the better class, who subscribe one hundred pounds a year towards the support of a chaplain, besides two hundred negroes who are also professed Protestants.

W. CHAMPNESS

PANAMA to SAN FRANCISCO

It was not necessary for us to wait long in Panama, as the California steamer "Orizaba" was just starting for San Francisco, distant from here more than four thousand miles. On re-embarking, we speedily found occasion to institute the most unfavorable comparisons between the British steamer in which we had crossed the Atlantic, and the one we were now on board of. We had fallen into the hands of a wealthy and almost irresponsible monopolist, the great Yankee ship-owner Vanderbilt, who, in 1860, bought up the previous opposition line of steamers from the Isthmus to California. Since that time he has had the passenger traffic almost exclusively in his own power, and has more than doubled the former fares, and greatly reduced the comforts and even necessaries of travel. Specially unfortunate were the poor steerage and second-class passengers. For, although the "Orizaba" was a large steamer, with three or four tiers of cabins, and galleries one above another, like the American river-boats, yet more than twelve hundred passengers were crowded into her, or double the number she could accommodate with any degree of comfort. Amongst the multitude on board were a number of poor German and Irish emigrants, who had just come into Panama from New York, having landed at Aspinwall from the "Northern Light," one of the American line to the Isthmus, on the

Atlantic side. These being, for the most part, ragged, money-less, and filthy, were a great addition to the discomfort and disturbance of the ship. Men, women, and children were huddled together, day and night, without regard to comfort or decency. Many and universal were the denunciations against the selfish monopolist ship-owner, and the threats of legal proceedings on arrival at San Francisco. But we afterwards learnt that the Californian newspapers had long protested the avaricious extortions and disreputable abuses of this line of steamers, but hitherto without obtaining redress, especially as those who bore the brunt of the annoyance were the poorer class of passengers, the saloon being comparatively well cared for. Besides, although the Americans talk loudly of their independence and freedom, their laws are not readily put in force against powerful and wealthy offenders. British impartiality in affording legal redress is little known across the Atlantic.

Finding that we were now hopelessly committed to fourteen days of great discomfort, we tried to make the best of it. Fortunately the weather continued very fine throughout, and the ocean was as smooth as glass; so that our vessel moved on as quietly and rapidly as a steam-yacht in the beautiful Mediterranean. We were informed that storms are very unusual in this part of the Pacific. Indeed, were it otherwise, the class of steamers we were in could not navigate it; being so high above the water, with their tiers of cabins, they would be very ill adapted for facing the mighty waves of the Atlantic storms.

Notwithstanding our sunshine and calm, we were so annoyed by our over-crowded condition, and still further aggrivated by the churlishness of the seamen and attendants, and by the wretched fare provided, that signs of something like a mutiny were apparent, even in spite of the ostentatious display of revolvers and bowie knives carried by the officers and others. We insisted on having some satisfaction or amelioration from the captain's hands, and, by our firmness and united feeling, at length obtained an improvement in our treatment for the remainder of the voyage.

In seven days we touched at Acapulco, on the Mexican coast, and half-way towards San Francisco. Here the steamer coaled, and the passengers were enabled to land for a few hours, and stroll about on *terra firma*. Immediately on our arrival, many small boats surrounded us, bringing out cargoes of melons, pine-apples, and bananas, which found a ready market on board. Many boys and youths in these boats amused us by their dexterity in diving deep for small silver coins, thrown into the sea by the passengers. It was astonishing to see how long they were able to remain under water. When we had finished coaling we resumed our voyage, pleased that, at any rate, half of it was now completed. It was a matter for sincere thankfulness that, in our excessively crowded and comfortless condition, and with so little regard for cleanliness as was manifested by the generality of both passengers and crew, no infectious fever or other disease broke out amongst us. Had it done so, probably hundreds of us would have speedily fallen victims to the avarice of our shipowner. The only objects of interest between Acapulco and San Francisco were the little flying-fish, several huge spouting whales, and thousands of porpoises, or "skip-jacks," as the sailers call them. These raced, dived, and leaped around us in countless numbers; now flinging themselves high above the water, then plunging suddenly out of sight, and presently cleaving the surface again with a bound, and following one another in rows and troops, as if bent on throughly amusing themselves and us.

At length, on the evening of the fourteenth day from Panama, we saw the long sand-hills which skirt the Pacific side of the narrow tongue of land, on the inner part of which the city of San Francisco is situated. Then, passing the lighthouses on the Farraleones rocks (haunts of sea-lions and myriads of sea-fowl), we crossed the bar and entered the Golden Gate just before midnight. This narrow channel, here less than a mile wide, connects with the Pacific the large and mountain-girt bay of San Francisco, which is eighty miles long by ten in breath —a noble inland water.

The current in the Golden Gate set so strongly outward, that although we passed through it easily by our steam-power, we observed a barque, with every inch of canvas spread, including studding-sails, and with a favorable wind astern, yet apparently remaining stationary for nearly ten minutes in the swift channel opposite the fort, whose white walls were shining in the full moonlight; and a fishing-boat seemed for a short time in little better plight, notwithstanding that its sails were fully outspread in "wing and wing" style.

As we emerged from the Gate into the bay, the upper portion of the city, Telegraph Hill, appeared before us. On it one large building was brilliantly lighted, within and without. This was recognised as the Chinese Joss-house. A "festival of lanterns" was being held by some of the Celestials, who form no inconsiderable portion of the inhabitants of the place. Presently, passing the the fortification of Alcatraz Island, we were abreast of San Francisco, glided into a warf, and, although midnight, were presently boarded by a throng of touters and hotel-messengers, each promising us "the best accommodation in the city." One of these we followed, and were presently seated in a light, neat two-horsed van, and driven off to an hotel, where we found comfortable quarters, which seemed doubly so by contrast with our wretched treatment whilst cramped and crowded during the fortnight on the "Orizaba."

SAN FRANCISCO

Being thus again on *terra firma,* we much enjoyed a four day's sojourn in the Golden City. Early next morning, on looking over it, we saw that it extends for about two miles along the side of a treeless three-crowned hill, up whose steep slopes its streets and houses ascend in successive terraces, approached in many cases by long flights of steps. The lower part of the city is built on piles, and projects nearly a quarter of a mile over the beach and shallower water. Here, as in other parts of San Francisco, the streets are not paved with stone, but planked with wood. In this lower town there are frequent deaths, from unwary persons falling, or being thrust, at night into the water, through some of the large openings occurring at intervals in the super-marine streets. Many murders have thus taken place.

But, by day, no scene is more stirring than the wharves. Here, on our first morning, we saw, swiftly gliding out into the bay, a large double-tiered steamboat, having a band of music playing cheerily to a pic-nic party of twelve hundred "Dashaways" (the Californian name for teetotallers, because they claim to "dash away the wine cup"). On they went for a day's excursion to Ravenswood, up the bay; but (accidents will happen) in a few hours the news was spreading that the unfortunate "Dashaways" had run aground on a sand-bank, half-way to their destination, in which uninteresting position they were detained till near nightfall. The evening newspapers contained sundry sly allusions to the accident being possibly owing to the presence on board of beverages less mild than coffee and lemonade.

W. CHAMPNESS

In 1848 San Francisco was a dull sandy village of a few "adobe" (or sun-dried mud) houses. Now it is a rapidly increasing city of a hundred thousand inhabitants, and possesses miles of busy streets, with elegant shops, large hotels, public libraries, museums, clubhouses, suburban villas, a telegraph across the continent, steam ferries, a street railway, and numerous handsome churches and chapels. The highest part of the city (Russian Hill) is three hundred feet above the wharves, and, in looking down the straight steep streets, there is everywhere presented a noble view over the broad bay and its islands and the sierra-like mountains beyond, on the Contra Costa side, behind which, again, rises the cleft summit of Monte Diavolo, three thousand feet high.

In the center of the city is the spacious Plaza, or Washington Square. Here is the Town Hall, over which is the great bell which, a few years ago, used to be rung at times to summon the Vigilance Committee, composed of many hundreds of the citizens, who had banded together to execute Lynch-law on such offenders as grossly set at defiance the imperfectly organized legal executive of the young state. On such occasions a brief public examination of the accused took place, and a few minutes decided his guilt or innocence; if the former, he was at once hung, in the presence of his arrestors and judges, "the sovereign people." This state of things has passed away, and evil-doers are left to the strong hand of the law in its now fully organized authority.

One of the things in San Francisco which immediately strike a stranger is the respectable appearance of the great mass of citizens. Almost every one appears well-dressed; the gentlemen wearing good broadcloth frock-coats, and wide-brimmed

VIEW OF SAN FRANCISCO

conical-crowned black hats, somewhat in the Italian style. Amongst the ladies one often observes the bright dark eyes and hair usually indicative, hereabouts, of Spanish extraction, especially when accompanied by the single flattened curl on each side of the forehead.

It is evident that the Californians live in a land where gold is plentiful. The visitor who has been accustomed to handling the small sovereigns of England, and the tiny gold dollars of the eastern states of the Union, looks with admiration on the large *rouleaux* of heavy twenty-dollar gold pieces, nearly the size of half-crowns, which he sees so freely transferred in the offices and banks of San Francisco. There is no copper currency in the state, except incidentally. The smallest coin is a "bit" or "dime" worth ten cents, or fivepence. A merchant, speaking to us of the currency, mentioned that a Bostonian, lately arrived, entered his store for some goods. A bill was made out, and the cash handed in. The merchant, thinking all was settled, returned to his accounts, but, seeing his customer waiting near the desk, asked him if there was any mistake. "Why, yes I guess there's them few cents change to pay." "Oh, my friend, I see you are a stranger in these parts," replied the man of business; "but, very well; when I meet with any cents, I'll keep them for you till you call again."

Since the outbreak of the Secession war, whilst the other States have been deluged with "greenbacks," California has firmly refused to adopt any other than a wholly metallic currency, and, being far away from the eastern States, it has not been deemed prudent to attempt to compel the adoption of paper. Although the prices of things in general are not so high here as in former years, yet they are much in excess of those paid for the same articles in Europe or the Atlantic States. But salaries and wages also range high. So do houses. A small dwelling of six or eight rooms, anywhere near the city, is considered to be reasonably rented at sixty dollars a month. Payments of rent, interest, and wages are usually reckoned by the month in California. Taxes are much heavier here (and throughout the States) than is commonly supposed to be the case by Englishmen.

The San Franciscans are generally very liberal in their contributions to objects of public interest, and in their charitable subscriptions. Not long ago they engaged Bayard Taylor, the well-known author and traveller, to come from New York (seven thousand miles by the usual sea route) to deliver a course of a few lectures, paying him handsomely, and franking all expenses. Again, one of the city congregations, requiring a minister, sent to a popular preacher in Boston, offering him six thousand dollars per annum to settle in San Francisco. Such a mark of appreciation did not fail to secure its object.

Amongst the truly cosmopolitan population of the city, fifteen thousand Chinese constitute a peculiar feature, especially as they retain their native customs, dress, and language, when amongst themselves. They are no favourites here, as they willingly work at much lower wages than whites, and are very clannish and selfish, as well as disagreeable in many of their habits.

The markets of San Francisco are much more convenient, as well as more imposing in the appearance of their stalls, than those of London. The butchers, for instance, have rows of neat counters, and their names inscribed above in large gilt letters. The fruiterers sit behind piled baskets of cauliflower, green peas, pineapples, mangoes, grapes, bananas, cranberries and strawberries. The latter, when in season, as they were at the time of our visit, are more abundant than in perhaps any other part of the world. Never before have we seen such a strawberry-and-cream-eating place as San Francisco. One cultivator, across the bay, has fifty acres laid out in this fruit alone. The mangoes and bananas are brought (in a fortnight) by fast-sailing schooners from the Sandwich Islands, which have become a sort of market-garden, as well as sea-side resort, for the inhabitants of the Golden City, though nearly two thousand miles away. But what is that distance to an American?

The bay furnishes abundance of oysters. From the other Pacific States of Washington and Oregon vegetables, game and coal are sent here. But California itself furnishes almost every kind of vegetable and mineral production. It is becoming one of the greatest corn-producing countries in the world, and already exports largely to Australia and Britain.

Although there are many prettily terraced gardens in and around the city, there are scarcely any trees in its vicinity, owing to the strong, but not cold winds which blow almost perpetually over it, and accumulate deep drifts from the numerous sand-hills in various parts of the suburbs. We shall always remember San Francisco as associated with whistling winds and ever-drifting sand, notwithstanding its otherwise agreeable and sunny climate. Its rocky neighbourhood is abundantly carpeted with flowers, especially the wild iris and pea, the bright yellow escholzia (or California poppy), the monkey-plant, and the flowering currant. Some of these, though wild here, are now cultivated amongst the ornaments of our English gardens.

The streets, running up-hill at right angles to the bay, are so steep that a stranger would think them very dangerous for driving; but this is not in reality the case, as the vehicles, usually of very light construction here go safely and easily up and down. The city cabs are far superior in style and appearance to those of London. They are brightly varnished and painted, have much glass, double seats, good harness and horses, and well dressed drivers.

The upper part of San Francisco is thickly covered with elegant villas and gardens, the latter generally entered by long flights of steps, and the former mostly furnished with neatly painted verandahs, outer galleries, and balustrades, in the Swiss style. The use of wood for building was for some years almost universal here; but the numerous and extensive conflagrations led to the enactment of a law requiring that, in future, all erections in the business throughfares of the city shall be of stone or brick. Consequently, elegant and solid structures are rapidly displacing the more fragile ones of early times. Each "block" of city land is four hundred and twelve feet long by two hundred and seventy-five in breath. The smaller plots are called "fifty vara lots," each being the sixth of a block, and equaling in area a square whose side is one hundred and thirty-seven and a half feet. A "vara" is the old Spanish or Mexican yard.

Amongst the principal buildings of San Francisco are the lofty two-towered cathedral of St. Francis, and the similarly fine one of St. Mary (both Roman Catholic); the Presbyterian, Unitarian, and Episcopalian churches; the Town Hall, the Mercantile Library and Club in Montgomery Street; the Freemasons' Institute, Custom House, and the Marine Hospital. The chief hotels are the "Metropolitan," the "Tehama House," and the "What-cheer House." One of the busiest establishments in the city is the large one of Wells, Fargo, and Co., who have the chief carrying freight, and parcel business of California and of the Pacific sea-board. They constitute in one firm that which Pickford's and the various parcels delivery companies of England form in the aggregate. Freight and luggage carriage are very heavy items here. At the time of our visit the charges for the transit of goods from San Francisco to New York, *via* the Isthmus, were at the rate of   5 12*s*. per hundred-weight, and by the Overland Express route even a dollar per pound.

An hour or two after the arrival of an eastern steamer (from New York), great is the rush to the post-office from all parts of the city, as there exists no postal delivery from house to house. (This applies to America generally). To facilitate the distribution of letters, and, at the same time, prevent repeated or unnecessary inquiries, the interior of the post-office is lined with hundreds of small pigeon-holes, all numbered, and each having a glass front; so that a person coming for letters can ascertain at once, by a glance at his box, whether there is anything for him. If so, he informs one of the clerks, and the box is opened for him.

The prospect of the future progress and importance of San Francisco is a grand one. Its bay is a remarkable exception to the almost universally open and unsheltered roadsteads of the Pacific sea-board; whilst its Golden Gate is the one means of navigable exit and entrance for the vast inland regions of California, Utah Nevada, and the Far West in general. Into this noble eighty-mile-long bay flow the Sacramento and San Joachin rivers, bringing down the treasures of the great central valley, which extends five hundred miles from north to south. Thus, naturally and permanently, San Francisco will continue unrivalled as the one great port and emporium of the Golden State and of the North Pacific sea-board of the Union.

VICTORIA - VANCOUVER'S ISLAND

EAVING SAN FRANCISCO by the steamer *Sierra Nevada,* in four days we reached Vancouver's Island and presently landed at Esquimault, a port four miles from the capital, Victoria. Leaving our luggage in charge of a black porter, to be brought on by cart, we walked to Victoria, which place we found crowded with emigrants on their way to British Columbia. On arrival at night at the "Colonial Hotel," we were glad to have a billiard-room alloted us for our lodging-place, as all the bed-chambers were filled. However, wrapping ourselves in blankets, we slept soundly on the floor, and so took our first repose in her Majesty's dominions on the Pacific.

The next day we spent walking about Victoria. It is a rapidly increasing town, of about five thousand inhabitants. Its appearance is not very prepossessing, as the houses are built in the most irregular manner, some being erected with their sides and gable-ends to the street, others at some distance back, and small log cottages side by side, "promiscuously" with large hotels and government offices. Most structures are wood, a few of brick, and pavements or side-ways being of wood. The position of Victoria, close to the Straits of Juan de Fuca, and on the route to the Fraser's River settlements, indicates a prospect of permanent and increasing importance. Its port of Esquimault has recently been selected as the naval station for British ships of war in the Pacific, in lieu of Valparaiso. Most of the land "lots" in the vicinity of the town have been bought up by speculators, especially from San Francisco, and remain for the present "locked," till a great rise in value tempts their owners to sell out to parties really wishing to build upon them and settle there. But many *bona fide* emigrants have purchased land from ten to twenty miles distant from Victoria, and are generally prospering in their operations, the soil hereabouts being rich and fertile, and its price at present cheap. Bullock-teams are in great demand for clearing the newly-bought land of timber and stumps: to draw the latter, eight or ten pair of beasts are often used.

After a few day's stay at Victoria we re-embarked on a steamer, for the concluding portion of our long voyage from England to British Columbia. This part of it, however, of short duration, as we reached our destination, New Westminster, the capital of British Columbia, the evening of the same day on which we left Vancouver's Island; the distance being only about eighty miles.

On our way we passed the celebrated island of San Juan, which is claimed both by the British and American governments, and is, for the present jointly held by soldiers of the two nations. A few years ago this disputed territory very nearly

HOUSES AT DOUGLAS

led to a war between them. Indeed, the avoidance of such a terrible calamity was owing, under Providence, to the courteous but firm refusal of Admiral Baynes and Captain Hornby to comply with the orders issued by Governor Douglas for commencing war. The latter has ceased to exercise ruling functions in these regions. A blessing it is for all concerned, when the military and naval representatives of Great Britain, in her distant dependencies, are so temperate and judicious as the two officers just alluded to, acting as dignitaries fully able to maintain her power, without compromising her honour or plunging her into the horrors of bloodshed.

New Westminster at present consists mainly of one very broad street. Like Victoria, its houses are mostly of wood, but with many temporary tents interspersed. Our party erected one of the latter forthwith, on landing. The first night under it was very comfortless, as heavy rain poured down and trickled through the canvas in streams. As we were bound "up country" to the diggings, our stay in the capital was of the shortest possi-

GAOL AT DOUGLAS

ble duration, and we were speedily again on board a river-boat for Douglas. The Fraser's River is a noble stream, flowing seven hundred miles, from the Rocky Mountains to the Gulf of Georgia, and for the most part, through scenery of wild grandeur. New Westminster is fifteen miles from its mouth, and situated above a wide extent of fertile but low-lying land on the estuary shores. In its neighbourhood promising mines of coal have been discovered.

As we steamed up the Fraser we had fine views on our right of the Cascade Ranges and Mount Baker, in the adjacent United States territory. Our intended route was by the line of lakes; for there are two ways of proceeding from New Westminster to the upper mining regions of the Fraser. One is by the direct line of the river for the whole distance, by way of Hope, Yale, Lytton, and Fort Berens, a point one hundred and eighty-eight miles from the sea; but, as the river is not navigable higher than Fort Yale, and as its valley beyond that point is of the most rugged and precipitous nature, the generally adopted route to the upper country is by a *détour* of lakes, rivers and portages, to the westward of the Fraser. Travellers by this line leave the latter river at the town of Carnarvon, and pass by the eight-mile-long Harrison River into Harrison Lake (thirty-seven miles in length), and so to Douglas; thence by Hot Springs, Lilooett Lake, Anderson River, and lakes Anderson and Seton, to Fort Berens, where the Fraser valley is again entered. The latter point is two hundred and twelve miles from the mouth of the river, by the route just indicated. Following the Fraser above Fort Alexander, or taking a more direct route across the mountains, and branching up the Quesnelle (a tributary from the east), the Cariboo diggings are reached. These lie north of

Lake Cariboo, which is itself north of Lake Quesnelle, and about four hundred miles from the mouth of Fraser's River. This explanation, with reference to the map, will assist in rendering our line of journeyings intelligible to the reader.

Our steamer, the "Colonel Moody," brought us in twenty

DRAWING OUT TREE-STUMPS WITH CATTLE

hours to Douglas, a wooden-built town on a small lake at the northend of the larger and mountain-girt Harrison Lake. But we need not thus specially characterize any one lake in British Columbia, for every lake, pond, stream, or valley hereabouts is embedded in mountains: the latter, like pine-trees and mosquitoes, are universal features and facts of the country.

Douglas derives its local importance from its position, at the commencement of the usual land transit up the country.

Its principal trade consists in supplying emigrants with provisions and necessaries, and in forwarding such to the diggings. Hotels are springing up rapidly, such as, for instance, the "Columbia House" and "Cariboo Restaurant." Very recently a daily line of stages has been established, to run in connection with the steamers on Lilooett and Anderson lakes; but this is since our visit, when the necessary roads were as yet not completed.

OUR START UP THE COUNTRY - PRELIMINARY DIFFICULTIES

At Douglas we united ourselves to a party of digging-bound emigrants (twelve in all), and laid in a supply of provisions for a four days' march of sixty miles, over a moutainous and rough track. Each of us charged himself with a burden of about fifteen pounds weight.

Whilst some of us were going from store to store on our commissariat errands, we espied one of our late fellow-passengers from England "in trouble," having been given in charge of a constable by the bar-man of the river-steamer, for passing bad money. Having found him to be a good sort of a fellow, so far as our previous travelling knowledge of him had extended, we were quite prepared to believe his protestations of innocence, or, at any rate, of ignorance, as to the coin (a sovereign) being a counterfeit one. The constable, however, had no option but to take him to the gaol till the nearest magistrate could be called upon to investigate the charge. One of our number, from sympathy, requested to be permitted to keep his unfortunate friend company. This application was acceded to, and both were locked up in the very primitive log-built gaol for about an hour, when the magistrate arrived on the spot, and heard the statements of all parties concerned. On carefully examining the coin, it was found to be a good one after all. This led to general indignation against the barman, who was now fairly open to a suspicion of having brought the charge in order to extort money, with a view to a compromise through the fears of the accused.

All this occasioned considerable delay at starting; and, on rejoining the rest of our party and explaining that, in company with a friend, we had been inspecting "one of the government buildings," they were much surprised at such ill-timed gratification of curiosity, until we related more particularly the true reason of our detention.

We now set off on our march, but only walked eight miles that day, as the route was exceedingly steep and rugged, and the heat oppressive. At nightfall we pitched our tent beside a clear mountain stream, where, after a hearty supper of bread, bacon, and tea, we slept soundly, in spite of mosquitoes which visited us during the night, and left indications of their attacks upon our limbs and faces. The next day we reached Hot Springs, so called from a stream of water which issues from the rocks here, and which is of a constant temperature too high to allow one's hand being dipped in it without scalding. At the inn we

THE START FROM LILOOETT

enjoyed what our Yankee companions called a "square meal," of the generally characteristic fare of the colony, bacon and beans; the latter are abundantly imported in barrels from the States. Here, also after our toilsome march, we indulged in a good wash, the only really cheap comfort obtainable in British Columbia.

Having further indulged in a meerschaum, we retired to our blankets for the night, and next morning, rising early, walked six miles before breakfast, between snow-covered pine-forested mountains, to Golledge Lake, where we rested during the mid-day heat (a common custom in America in summer). In the afternoon we proceeded to Lilooett by road, and a small steamer. Before reaching the latter we found our route interrupted by a rapid stream, fifty feet wide and four deep. Another party coming up, and having amongst them several Canadian woodmen, a tree was forthwith cut down, so as to fall athwart the river. Thus we crossed with our baggage dry. Several, however, were not so fortunate, but slipped into the stream; and one person narrowly escaped drowning, as the current was very strong. Subsequently we frequently met with similar adventures.

LILOOETT - A FRESH START

On the third day from Douglas we arrived at Lilooett, a young town, finely situated on a plain surrounded by lofty mountains, snow-covered even at midsummer; for it was now the 14th of June. Some attempts at gold-mining were being carried on here, chiefly by Chinese: their earnings were about three dollars a day.

We here held a council respecting our further route; and, after being informed of the rugged and mountainous nature of the trails from here to Cariboo (two hundred and fifty miles distant), and also of the very high price of provisions further up the country, we determined to lay in a large stock of flour, bacon, and beans, and engage a team of seven horses for our now enlarged party of twenty comrades. We further hired the services of an experienced California packer, who undertook to accompany us and securely pack our supplies on the beasts from time to time, at a uniform charge of thirty cents (fifteen pence) per pound on the whole weight of baggage. At this rate we had each to disburse about forty-five shillings, in addition to our purchase-money for the provisions, and also after our former expenditure for the supplies at Douglas, much of which still remained. The prices here were thirty-five cents per pound for bacon, thirty cents per pound for beans, and twenty-five cents per pound for flour. Further up country charges were still higher. An income of two hundred and fifty pounds per annum, in British Columbia, will not nearly produce the comfort which one hundred pounds would in England.

We unanimously agreed to take the Brigade Route, or Middle Trail, as affording at intervals abundance of water, good camping-ground, and plenty of grass for the horses. The operation of packing a team of horses or mules with baggage requires great skill, and is a long and tedious affair. The average burden put on each horse is three hundred pounds weight. Besides provisions, our cooking utensils (obtained at Lilooett) were thus carried. Altogether we found our expenses here much greater than we had anticipated; and this is universally the experience of those who come to British Columbia.

The horses used for pack-trains are mostly bred on the mountains of Oregon and California; and, though very restive at the first imposition of a burden, soon become tractable and

CROSSING A RIVER ON A FELLED TREE

quiet, finding their efforts at throwing off their pack only result in weariness and blows. They are sold in San Francisco for about eight pounds each.

Our route from Lilooett lay across the mountains to the Fraser River valley, near Lytton; thence up the wild and awful ravines in the district of the Thompson River, passing Loon Lake; and thence north, near Green and Axe lakes, to William's Lake. This portion of our journey, being a distance of nearly two hundred miles, occupied sixteen days, Sundays not included, as we were truly glad of a Sabbath rest.

SCENERY OF BRITISH COLUMBIA

Some portions of our route lay across mountain ranges, from whose summits we enjoyed most magnificent views, and down whose steep pine-forested sides we had to lead our horses singly, and with the utmost care. When on more level ground it was only necessary to lead the foremost one, and the rest would follow in regular file.

In other parts of the journey, especially in the river gorges, our track conducted us along the most frightful precipices. There was no help for this, as we could select no route more passable. Such dangerous travelling is a characteristic of British Columbia, Oregon, and Washington Territory. Their rivers flow oftentimes through dark and awful gorges, whose rocky sides tower perpendicularly from a thousand to fifteen hundred feet. By a series of zigzag paths, often but a yard in width, man and beast have to traverse these scenes of grandeur. Sad and fatal accidents often occur, and horses and their owners are dashed to pieces on the rocks below, or drowned in the deep foaming waters rushing down the narrow defiles from the vast regions of mountain snow melting in the summer heat.

"No country in the world affords more romantic scenes. The mountains bounding them rise in stately grandeur, often-

MOUNTAIN ROADS

times far above the clouds; now presenting their nude sides, paved with dark masses of frowning rocks, or proud forests of evergreen lawns, flowery dales and sterile wastes, to overlook the perennial beauty and matchless fecundity at their feet; while the lesser eminences, with their deep ravines, o'erhanging cliffs, and shadowy recesses, tell the place where the storm-winds recruit their forces and the zephyrs creep in to die."

Fortunately for ourselves, we escaped any serious accidents amid these wild scenes. But our progress was necessarily slow in such parts: only from six to eight miles a day in several cases. The backs of several of our poor beasts became very sore. This, again caused delays, and the utmost care in packing and adjusting the burdens. Not unfrequently our horses stumbled and fell. Our packer several times beat them harshly, attributing it all to their temper; and we had to interpose to prevent cruelty. Neither did we escape aches and gallings in addition to our weariness. Some of our party had equipped themselves with thick Wellington boots, which were now found to be ill adapted for travel like ours. The best foot-gear is a strong lace-up shoe, well covering the ankle. This affords much support, is neither too heavy nor too hot, and can be adapted to the varying size of the feet, which are sure to swell on such a trying and protracted exercise of pedestrianism.

At intervals we came upon fertile meadow-land, covered with a kind of high rye-grass, reckoned a superior herbage here, although it would be deemed very coarse in England. No other country can be compared with the United Kingdom for the fineness and softness of its grass. Neither America nor the continent of Europe can show such lawn-like meadows as those of our home islands. Whenever we encamped in these green spots, we and our beasts were specially pestered with mosquitoes. They visited us in myriads, piercing even through our very blankets. In some districts, such as Loon Lake, they were so intolerably worrying, that our animals would doubtless have been driven stark mad had we stayed long there at that time of the year.

THE INDIANS OF BRITISH COLUMBIA

As, in the course of our pilgrimage up the country, we repeatedly fell in with small parties of Indians, a few words respecting them will not be out of place here.

The native races of British Columbia exist in a condition of even greater degradation and squalor than the other aboriginal tribes of the Far West. Many of them inhabit holes and caves; others move about and erect temporary tents or huts of bark. We came upon a small party of them thus encamped by an ice-cold mountain stream near William's Lake. They are exceedingly filthy in their mode of life, swarm with vermin, are very licentious, superstitious, and cruel. Mr. Duncan G. F. Macdonald states, in his valuable and interesting work on British Columbia, that he has seen no less than thirty scalps in one of their wigwams! Truly "the dark places of the earth are full of the habitations of cruelty."

The Indians living along the shores of the Gulf of Georgia (both in British Columbia and Vancouver's Island) flatten the heads of their children by placing them, whilst very young, in wooden troughs, over the upper part of which a board is bound, so as to press upon the as yet tender forehead, and permanently flatten it. The effect of this imaginary adornment is to impart, in the eyes of a European, an expression something akin to idiotcy.

The Indians of these regions derive their chief subsistence from the fine salmon of their clear streams, and from the abundant waterfowl of their rocky inlets and estuaries. The tribes further inland are often pinched with hunger in the intervals between their rude feasts on bear-flesh, venison, and the numerous wild berries of their bushy plains and mountain thickets. They keep their animal food till is is absolutely putrid, preferring to eat it thus.

Not far from the encampment just alluded to we observed an Indian burial ground. Often only one corpse is deposited, and so left in its solitary slumber, either buried at a little depth beneath the earth, and staked round, or raised on poles, or amongst the branches of a tree, and so left to bleach and moulder drearily in the storms and sunshine of the wilds. The former possessions of the deceased, as his gun or arrows, kettle and blanket, are also brought and ranged around his remains. Death would be inflicted by his survivors on any one found plundering these relics. They are rarely if ever meddled with, even by the boldest Indian.

One of our comrades, once travelling in the wilderness,

ROUTE OVER FALLEN TREES

saw in the top of a high tree what appeared to be the large nest of some bird. Curiosity led him to climb up and inspect it; but, before reaching it, he discovered it to be the remains of some poor Indian, whose relatives had taken the trouble to bring him, after death, to so strange a resting-place, secure, as they supposed, from the desecrating paw of wandering bear or wolf.

WILLIAM'S LAKE - *Increased Difficulty of the Route*

William's Lake (also called Columetza) is about forty miles south of Fort Alexander. It is surrounded by some comparatively fertile land, and farming to some extent is carried on. We were truly glad to rest awhile at an inn here. Immediately on our arrival we ordered a "square meal," and an ample supply of fresh beef, beans, cabbage, pies, milk, tea and coffee was set before us, to which we did justice in a manner which we should have been almost ashamed for our English friends to witness. It is truly astonishing what an appetite is developed by the arduous travelling in this country. Solid meals of animal food, which at home would suffice for the day, are here requisite several times within a similar period, and at a fearful expense; but nothing can be accomplished otherwise. Thus, our meal above mentioned cost three half-dollars, or six shillings, each.

A little rest here was also most welcome to our poor horses, now reduced to six. Tom, our Californian packer, washed their sore backs frequently with Castile soap, as this application is found very efficacious. We were not much encouraged by the accounts here received from some parties of miners returning from the Cariboo diggings. They reported a general failure of success, and an awful condition of the route further up. Indeed, after hearing the complaints of our travelling difficulties thus far, they only laughed at us, saying, "You've not even reached the bad tracks yet." And we soon had reason to believe them; for, almost immediately after leaving William's Lake we found that we had exchanged bad for worse, in the matter of routes: our horses were often plunged up to the belly in swamps and mud. British Columbia is truly a horse-killing country. At other times we dragged our burdens heavily up steep and forested mountains. Then, again, we met frequently with rapid and deep streams, where, in the absence of bridges, we had to wade or otherwise attempt (*nolens, volens*) all manner of Blondin-like performances, and often at the risk of life and limb. Repeated practice, however, enabled us to perform feats of climbing, leaping, and crawling which formerly would have seemed utterly impossible to us. We now remarked to one another our belief that, if St. Paul's Cathedral were in British Columbia, we could safely walk round the steep side of its lofty dome, provided there was a trail of a foot wide on it.

At Deep Creek, ten miles from William's Lake, seven of our comrades dilinquished all further attempt to reach their proposed destination, being utterly discouraged by the excessive difficulties of the way, and the unvarying tale of disappointment told by the parties of returning and unsuccessful miners. Truly, the numbers of these poor broken-down fellows, with their pale,

pinched faces and tattered rags, eloquent of hunger and pover-
ty, were enough to dishearten all of us together; for hundreds
of such passed us during our journey, in parties of from two to a
score. Sorely tempted as we were to yield to despair, yet some
of us resolved to brave out to the end, feeling that, having come
thus far, and being almost in sight of the land of our hopes, we
would rather leave our bones there than abandon our object
when so near its goal.

Having resumed our journey, with numbers thus diminished, we soon reached a rude log-bridge across a torrent in a
ravine. Here one of our horses fell over into the water. Our
packer, by means of a rope, hoisted it up, and, nearly drowned
as it was beat it savagely to make it move on; but the plunge
and the blows after so much slavery of exertion, were too much,
and the wretched beast died close to the bridge where it had
slipped. And thus miserably perish hundreds of horses and
mules along this weary track. Often we had to hurry past their
offensive carcases, left by the side of our narrow ways.

We thought we had now reached the lowest possible depth
of difficulty; but not so: for, after miles of deep mud and
swamp, we came to a region where, for an extent of many miles,
the earth was covered with innumerable thousands of dead and
fallen trees, lying across each other in inextricable confusion,
and in every conceivable position; whilst myriads of others were
still standing, but leafless, dead, and bleached, almost as white

as snow. This strange scene had a ghostly and weird appearance, as if Nature had set her curse upon the region. We were necessitated to travel over these fallen trees, stepping from trunk to trunk, for a distance of ten miles. As may be supposed, this rendered us intensely fatigued and leg-weary; for it was, throughout, a series of acrobatic performances. Often we slipped between the fallen trunks and were nearly lost to view, having sunk two feet in a thick black swamp. Whenever one of us became "bogged," he had to call for help, and was drawn out bodily by his comrades from his unpleasant position. And the difficulties with our poor beasts were here worse than ever; in fact, all but insurmountable. After many such mishaps, and many "spells" for breath, we at length got over this remarkable stage of our journey, and were most truly glad to find ourselves once more on dry, open ground.

STILL MORE DISCOURAGEMENT

As we proceeded we met other parties of returning miners, who advised us at least to wait awhile before proceeding to the diggings, until the melting of the snow should have diminished, and the route become less muddy and swampy. All agreed in admitting that there was abundance of gold at Cariboo, if it could only be got at.

One morning, after our usual night's halt, we were dismayed at the tidings that four of our horses had stampeded, leaving us only one to proceed with. We were unanimously convinced that our packer had played us foul; but he stoutly and seriously persisted in his utter innocence of any complicity in the loss of the animals. At any rate, there was no remedy for us, as, by the terms of our bargain, we had "cashed down" before starting, and he had handed over the dollars to his partner at Lilooett. Further, we could prove no charge against him. So, in very poor plight indeed, we had to proceed as best we could. Two days afterwards we found our four horses in one of the valleys ahead; they were none the worse for their rest. It was no wonder the jaded beasts had run off; but it was now evident that our packer had had no share in the matter.

At night we heard the growling of the cinnamon bear, and fired off salutes from our revolvers, by way of warning and alarm. After quitting our encampment in the morning, we shortly passed a stake, on which was inscribed, "A young man is buried here; being killed by a bear at this spot." For ourselves, however, we found the mosquitoes far more annoying than any bears.

Four or five miles further on our way we came upon another grave, with a board over it, on which was written, "William S——, aged 23." This saddened us, for we recognised the name as that of one of our fellow-voyagers from Panama, where he had arrived from New York, on his way to the diggings; and a very pleasant companion we had found him. On subsequent inquiry respecting his death, we found that it had only just occured before our arrival at the spot, and was owing to his incautious use of fire-arms. On arising from his night's rest on some blankets (under which he had placed a cocked revolver before sleeping), he had, in drawing it from its position, caught the trigger in the folds. By the discharge of the weapon he was shot dead instantly, to the astonishment and grief of his companions (three Cornish miners), who dug a grave for him there, and, carefully wrapping his blankets round him, left him to his long rest.

Accidents with fire-arms are of frequent occurrence in this country, through the inexperience of their possessors. Furthermore, revolvers are of little or no use here; the same weight of good worsted stockings would be far more serviceable. Although we carried revolvers with us on our journey hither, we should not consider it necessary to take them a second time; and we have generally observed that those persons who are the least skilful in the use of fire-arms are the most ostentatious in their display, and the most careless in handling them.

Soon after this sad spectacle of a recent comrade's grave, we reached Beaver Lake, which, like William's Lake, is surrounded by some tolerable Farming land. Here we saw turnips, cabbages, and radishes being cultivated, but, as yet, had met with no potatoes in this country.

British Columbia is not, in general suited for agricultural

development. The climate is excessively cold in winter, and in summer the floods from the mountains inundate some of the valleys to a depth of many feet. During the latter season the days are fine and bright, and warmer than in England, but yet are often succeeded by frosty nights—a suddenness of change very unfavourable to many kinds of vegetation. But the climate suits the sturdy mountain trees: the cedar, the oak, and the pine. Some of the latter here often attain a diameter of twelve feet, and a height of more than two hundred feet—especially the Douglas Pine. Even these giants of the mountains are sometimes burst asunder by the extreme cold of the British Columbian winter. It is truly a savage region.

Our next stopping-place was Little Lake. Here we were only ten miles from the Forks of Quesnelle, but these ten miles were amongst the worst; for, in traversing part of the distance, we were again plunged at times to the middle in swamps and between protrate dead trees lying across the route. After thus proceeding we met a strange and very unexpected spectacle— a pack-train of camels. They had been brought across the Pacific, at considerable expense, from the Amoor River, in Asia, by some Yankee speculators, but had proved a very poor investment. Indeed, here they reminded one of "fish out of water," by the very fact of their wading through swampy ground; inasmuch as the camel is specially adapted for a dry and sandy region only. Their large and expanding feet are most unsuited to deep mud; whereas the small and solid hoofs of the American mule occasion much less difficulty in such circumstances.

The clayey, swampy ground hereabouts extended even to the top of the mountains, where we had least expected to find it;

TO THE DIGGINGS AND FROM THE DIGGINGS

but, owing to some breadth of table-land there, we were disappointed. The semi-liquid clay in the pans of the brick and tile-works at home may afford the reader an idea of our route here. Thus, after twenty-one day's wading and stumbling, sliding and climbing, we reached our next principal stage—the Forks of Quesnelle.

THE FORKS OF QUESNELLE

THIS PLACE IS THE principal depot for provisions and materials for the mines, being located about fifty miles from the gold region of Antler Creek and adjacent part of Cariboo. The town at the Forks consists of general stores (mostly kept by Jews) and drinking-shops: it is prettily situated, and the climate is milder than in many parts of the surrounding region.

Here, too, we met with many returned miners encamped. Their accounts were deplorable, and their manifest condition confirmed the worst. Yet, here again, all admitted the existence of rich gold deposits at the mines. Their complaints were of the excessive dearness of provisions and stores, the impossibility of getting many necessaries, even for money; and, beyond all, the intolerable difficulties of the soil and the tracks. Whilst waiting here we saw two packers return from the mines. One of them carried with him a bell, such as is fastened to the foremost mule of a pack. Suspecting some disaster, we inquired after their animals, and received for reply a statement that they had started hence to Antler Creek with a train of thirty mules, not one of which had reached the destination, all having fallen down, at different places, into the precipitous ravines, along the perpendicular sides of which the narrow trails led them. Sometimes

HUTS AND STORES AT ANTLER'S CREEK

a single such stumble involves a fall of a thousand feet. This, to an animal burdened with three hundred pounds weight of goods, is, of course, certain death. Yet many of the poor creatures do not die immediately after falling, but linger awhile in horrible torture, far beyond the possibility of aid or access by their owners, who are compelled to leave them to die, and to suffer the utter loss of the property fallen with them.

In consequence of the continual and general discouragement from nearly every miner we met at this and previously visited places, the majority of our party now relinquished their purpose of pushing on to the diggings, although arrived as at their very threshold. Eventually only about eight of the seventy emigrants who left Southampton with us for Cariboo reached that destination. The difficulties of travel here are truly stupendous; and every one capable of giving an opinion agrees that no country in the world can be compared with British Columbia in this respect. We had constantly to experience the utter fallaciousness of certain writers who have sent home glowing reports of this land and of its advantages. Misled by such gross misrepresentations, thousands have bitterly rued the day that they ever landed here, and more than a few have left their bones in these solitary wildernesses and vast gorges.

We met numbers of strong and active men, who would have gladly given their hard labour even for their food, without any other remuneration; but their services found no employ. And it is a fact that we saw a crowd of men standing around a butcher's slaughter-house waiting for the offal of a bullock to be thrown amongst them. This they seized like a pack of hounds. Hundreds, after working like slaves, and expending all their little capital, have had to retrace their weary way down to the coast, with scarcely rags enough to cover them, obliged to tie a bit of sacking round their bleeding feet, and to sell their blankets for a very little bread. (The price of a half-quartern loaf was now six shillings.)

Our small party reached Keithleys' Creek in two days from the Forks, passing along the shore of Cariboo Lake. There we paid half a dollar each to cross the deep stream in a boat; and it was money well expended, as it saved us a weary circuit of three miles—no trifling matter when burdened with fifty or sixty pounds of baggage. Keithleys is one of the most dull and gloomy places on the route, consisting of rude log-shanties of the roughest description. We stayed several days here. The little stock of provisions we had brought with us (of beans, bacon, and flour) was eagerly bid for by the store-keepers. We were offered twenty sovereigns for about half a hundred-weight of this supply; but we would have refused double that sum; for gold is not to be preferred at the risk of starvation. Not one pound of flour was obtainable at Keithleys, except that which we had brought. Beans and bacon were here "the staff of life."

In the year 1860 much gold was found at Keithleys, and extensive mining operations were set on foot. A very heavy outlay was incurred for "flumes" (the Californian name for long wooden conduits to bring water to the diggings), water-wheels, and sluice boxes, etc. All this "plant" was swept away in a few hours by a flood, since which the place has not been the scene of much mining effort.

We now set out once more, and for our last stage up-country, being bound for Antler Creek, about twenty-five miles from Keithleys. The weather was most inclement: rain, sleet, and snow. In two days we reached our destination —the diggings; and a cheerless spot it was: everywhere mud and water, and the atmosphere bitterly cold, although in the summer season; for we were now amongst the inland mountains.

AT CARIBOO - THE DIGGINGS

So we reached Cariboo at last; for Antler Creek is one of the principal places in the Cariboo district. We found the miners generally as dispirited as the accounts received on our upward journey had represented them to be. Many were trooping away. Yet both here and at the neighbouring diggings of William's Creek, Lake House, Lightning Cañon, Last Chance, Peterson's, Davis's, and Cunningham's Claims, much gold was being found. At the latter place two hundred ounces per diem were said to be taken out. Indeed,there is good reason to believe that this season fully a ton of gold has been here obtained. But at what cost! The expenses are enormous; for the mines hereabouts are not mere surfaceworks, like many of those in Australia and California, but involve heavy outlay and deep exploration.

We were also informed that the single item of candles amounted to sixty dollars per diem in one mine. Skillful miners were obtaining wages of from eight to ten dollars a day, and working in successive relays, day and night. But then, these were experienced men, chiefly from Cornwall and California. The general run of immigrants could neither accomplish such work, nor meet with the opportunity of being employed. The above wages may appear very high; but it must be remembered that the price of food alone amounted on an average to five or six dollars per day for each man, besides other heavy incidental and necessary expenses. Then, too, the work is very toilsome, being labour under the cold dripping of water from leaky flumes, and with clothes saturated with slush and water from head to foot. The mine proprietors have necessarily to incur excessive expense in the erection of flumes, the carrying out of sluice-boxes, and the sinking of shafts; and many have made all this outlay in vain, not succeeding in striking on the right place for the precious deposit. Hundreds have sunk their "bottom dollar" before reaching the golden ore. Altogether, the experience of gold-mining in British Columbia hitherto has been some brilliant success, but much, very much disheartening failure, and the latter far preponderating over the former.

For ourselves, we "prospected" about Antler and its neighbourhood for a fortnight, but to no profit. Gold was evidently around and beneath us, abundantly; but there seemed little or no hope of our being more fortunate in obtaining it than the majority of other miners. So at length, after mutual deliberation and calculation we resolved to do what multitudes had done before us—turn back again. Sorely disappointed, but yet not utterly cast down, we began to retrace our steps over the same fatiguing route by which we had arrived; and on July 18th we had already returned to Keithleys, where it was a real consolation to feel that we had finally left behind us the worst twenty-five miles in the country.

LOST ON A NEW TRAIL

Our next backward stage was Beaver Lake again, where we came upon a small camping party of three of our fellow-shipmates by the "La Plata," bound for the mines, but taking it very leisurely; far too much so, as it seemed to us, for they were letting slip the best part of the year for mining, and, indeed, the only three months in which much work can be done, viz., July, August, and September. Like ourselves, they had met with many vicissitudes fo travel. They had packed with only two horses, which were often missing in the mornings, and so involved many an hour's delay. Our friends were surprised to see us returning; as, knowing that so many others had done so, they had concluded that we, at any rate were amongst the fortunate ones. Their small party had got on better than many other larger companies, through their great unanimity and willingness to oblige one another. Many parties have been broken up and greatly delayed by grumblers and unreasonable members. Yet, truly, there is ample palliation for grumbling, as the mosquitoes alone are here plague enough to try the patience of the firmest; but it is positively worse than useless to yield to the discouragements, or complain of the privations, as all have to share and share alike. Every one must be willing to take any share of toil, whether it appears his allotted portion or not; on no other terms can pleasant companionship be maintained.

A new trail had just been explored from Beaver Lake to Bridge Creek, below Spring Valley, thus missing William's Lake entirely, and so shortening the route by thirty miles, and reducing it to seventy instead of a hundred. This was an important consideration for us, as carrying packs on our shoulders, and the weather being here again extremely hot. We calculated that we could walk the distance in four days, and provisioned ourselves accordingly, not taking more than we considered necessary for the time, as we knew that further down the country prices were much lower; whereas here, at Beaver Lake, flour was now more than half-a-crown a pound.

We missed our way more than once for short distances on this trail, and then lost our bearings altogether. We did not meet a creature for days, and scarcely saw even a bird. But the mosquitoes on this route surpassed in numbers and annoyance all that we had previously met or heard of. Neither fire nor smoke appeared to avail us against their multitudinous swarms.

On the fourth evening from Beaver Lake we had consumed all our stock of provisions except tea, of which we had brought a good supply. We were now weary, anxious, hungry, without food, and irritated to desperation by the mosquitoes. After making tea, which was some refreshment, although unaccomanied by any solid nourishment, we tried to sleep, but could not, in consequence of our blood-sucking tormentors. Long before morning we arose, lighted fires around ourselves in all directions, lay down again, and, covering heads and faces with our blankets, obtained some measure of repose. By-and-by, after another recourse to our milkless, sugarless tea, we again started on our uncertain track, and must have walked nearly twenty miles on this the fifth day, when evening again overtook us. For the fourth or fifth time since morning we took tea, and then succeeded another wretched night, followed by another purely liquid breakfast; soon after which we were startled by a distant noise, which we found to proceed from two runaway horses stampeded by the mosquitoes. So ravenously hungry were we, that we sallied after them with gun and pistol, hoping to be able to shoot one, and secure some steaks, but failed in this attempt. The latter food would now have seemed more delicious to us than any good English beef had ever been. It was now the sixth morning; the sun shone brightly, and the face of nature was outstretched before us in summer splendour; but we were intensely anxious and careworn. At this juncture most welcome relief met us in a thicket of bushes,

A FARMSTEAD IN BRITISH COLUMBIA

bearing abundance of ripe fruit, here called the "service-berry,"
the flavour of which is a mixture of that of the sloe and the

grape. Having eagerly sustained ourselves with them, our spirits rose considerably, and we regarded this timely succour as a mark of Providential care for our preservation. After several tea-drinkings, another night found us still lost in the wilderness. But for our tea we must have utterly broken down. We could not have believed, except from experience, that this beverage had such power to support exhausted nature. At length, on the next day, the seventh from our last start, and the third of our fast, we re-entered a well-beaten trail, and the same evening arrived at Spring Valley, where, at such a solitary road-side house, we found both the food and rest of which we now stood so urgently in need.

SPRING VALLEY

The district in which we had now arrived was a fine rolling country, not very hilly, and covered at this season with luxuriant natural grass, fit for the scythe, and yielding about a load and a half per acre. It is intermixed with good tares. Many parts hereabouts are of rich flat meadow-land, suitable for a race-course or a cricket-ground; but cattle could hardly exist here at present in summer, one may presume, on account of the intolerable pest of mosquitoes. Not all the gold in British Columbia would have tempted us to take up our residence in such a beplagued spot. Although, in many respects, this district is (unlike other parts of the country) eminently adapted for agriculture, yet its distance from the mines, the absence of roads, and the intervening mountains all around, preclude the probability of successful farming operations until after a period of many years.

More wild animals are observed hereabouts than in other parts of British Columbia; such as the bear, deer, lynx, and wolf. The loud deep noise of the drumming grouse, and the sharp tap of the small golden-winged woodpecker, often fall upon the ear; whilst the beaver and the otter prey on the numerous fish of the clear valley streams. In the forests, and on the mountains, the eagle and the large-horned owl are the chief amongst the feathered tribes; but there is an almost total absence of singing-birds. There is a characteristic abundance of waterfowl on lake and river. One misses, too, the numerous flowers of California, England, and other lands; for here are very few native blossoms of any kind. Heavy, sombre, lofty pine and oak, together with mountain and gorge, are the chief features in the Columbian landscape; but whatever of the picturesque is here to be found can nowhere be seen to greater advantage than in the vicinity of Spring Valley and Bridge Creek (a small settlement seven miles further down the trail). At the latter place we stopped a day or two, and re-provisioned for a fresh start. The owner of some cows here furnished us with abundance of milk and good coffee during our stay— a welcome change after our late style of living.

On conversing about our torments by mosquitoes, we were informed of a recent incident, which strikingly exemplifies the ferocious cruelty of the Indians. One of the natives, having in some way given offence to the chiefs of his tribe, was by them ordered to be stripped naked and bound hand and foot to a tree in a valley, and so left to be killed by the mosquitoes. In fifteen hours life was extinct; but he had become quite mad soon after being tied up. A white man must have expired much sooner.

In this part of our journey we again fell in with small parties of Indians. Their squaws (called by them "clootchmen") were heavily burdened by their lords, some of whom have three wives. Woman is universally regarded as a slave by these savages, as by those of other wild regions.

The bodies of the native tribes in British Columbia appear very thick-set, powerfully built, and well adapted to the arduous and rugged nature of their land. Their feet are peculiarly thick-skinned, and their toes very short and strong. They entertain a decided aversion to the Americans, whom they term Boston men, but are favourably disposed toward King George men, as the English are still termed amongst the wild tribes of the north-west.

Having recruited after our three days' fast, we proceeded on our downward route; passing near Axe Lake, and along the shores of Green Lake, thence over the mountains to Loon Lake, and then by Scotty's Ranche into the valley of the Thompson

River. We resolved to take no more short cuts by unknown trails, having now lernt, by fresh and impressive experience, the truth of the old motto that "a known road is always the nearest." We continued to fall in with parties of unsuccessful miners. Near Bridge Creek we passed one who looked as if he had lain down to die, being pale, emaciated, worn out, and without a blanket or any covering but a few old rags. We were ourselves so scantily furnished with provisions that we were unable to render him much service. He made no complaint, and asked no relief; knowing well, as every one in this country does, that, as a rule, travelling miners are unable to do more than grapple with their own troubles. But, where they are able to help one another, the miners are a very generous set of men, as we had many opportunities of observing.

Every one who comes to British Columbia must reckon upon hardship as inevitable, even to the most successful gold-seeker. The miner never sleeps in a bed for months, or even years, but wraps himself in a blanket, and lays himself on the bare ground, or at best under a tent or log-hut. Many become so accustomed to this as afterwards to prefer such repose, at least for a time, to that in the softest bed. Then, again, one's blanket and clothes are often wet through, and a night's rest in such imparts less of repose than of stiffness. The latter must then be "taken out" by a twelve or fifteen miles' walk. One thing to be safely counted on here is an excellent appetite. We had no murmuring at our food. It was always done to our liking. No portion carved or helped was refused as being overdone, or underdone, or not the part preferred; nor were we more particular about the incidentals of the cooking and serving. Soon after our arrival in this country, and when starting upward for the mines, we were dining with a large party at a boarding-house, when a young man at the table, having disposed of his first course of bacon and beans, asked for a clean plate and some pudding. This request produced a general laugh at his expense, as it clearly proclaimed him a "new chum." The landlord good-humouredly remarked, "If I give you a clean plate, it will certainly be the last you will have in this country—at any rate for a long time." The young man was often afterwards jocularly reminded of his unminerlike fastidiousness; all of which he took in very good part, and soon learned to eat, like his comrades, with hearty relish out of the lid of an old tin saucepan. A shovel is often used as a plate at a digger's dinner. A prospecting-pan forms a first-rate dish for beans and bacon. It is one of the most useful articles one can bring here, and is light of carriage—a very important consideration.

TO SCOTTY'S RANCHE

We were reluctant to leave Bridge Creek, for it was one of the most pleasant and least foreign-like of our stopping-places. Its open meadow-land and small lakes abounded in wild-fowl;

but scarcely any of the latter fell to our lot, although we had revolvers and a double-barrelled gun with us. The latter is one of the most useless articles a miner can bring with him to this country. It is of scarcely any value for protection, but may, on the other hand, provoke assault and robbery. It forms a heavy and burdensome encumbrance, which may be carried up and down the country for seven or eight hundred miles, with very rare opportunities of procuring its owner even a scanty meal. Some miners who brought guns here were sensible enough to throw them away after carrying them in vain for fifty or a hundred miles up the rocky valleys and precipitous trails.

The total amount of game bagged by our party during our long journey up and down was two grouse, three ducks, and two squirrels. We much regretted that we had brought no fish-hooks with us. They would have been truly valuable, especially when at the lakes; and they are very light to carry. The smaller sizes are most useful here, as trout are the most abundant inland fish. They are generally from half a pound to four pounds weight. There are also many salmon in some of the rivers.

We were delighted with the picturesque scenery of Green Lake. Its glassy waters, scarcely ruffled by a ripple, were dotted with small islands covered with clusters of pine-trees. Large water-fowl, especially wild geese, were gliding over its plate-glass-like surface. We could only look at them, for they were far beyond the reach of our double-barrel, and, could we have shot them, we were unable to lay hold of them unless a strong wind had blown them towards us. So, in the absence of game and fish from our reach, we were content at evening to strike a fire, boil our pot of tea, and fry some beans, bacon, and flapjacks (or pancakes of flour and water with a little fat)—a sumptuous feast to us after our day's march, and followed by a quiet, dreamy, pleasant meerschaum before turning in for the night's sound repose.

Next day we had again very mountainous tracks and fatiguing climbing. We were visited at our next encampment by a rattlesnake, which we killed. It had fifteen rings in its rattle, and was therefore seventeen years old; its length was about three feet and a half. They move but slowly. The one here killed was evidently trying to get into our tent. They are fond of warmth, and will readily creep into blankets and folded clothes.

Four miles of our route hereabouts was through a peculiarly tenacious mud, which clung to us like bird-lime, and rendered our transit most wearisome. Having passed this, we soon reached the narrow but romantic Loon Lake. It seemed alive with fish; but here, again, we were only tantalized by the sight, having no hooks to catch any. The remainder of the distance to Scotty's was made by a comparatively easy trail.

On our arrival there, we found it a single wooden house with one small window. It is a much frequented place for rest and refreshment, being on one of the main trails to and from the diggings. Its surrounding scenery is of the grandest description: mountains and precipices are piled together in magnificent ruggedness and confusion.

Scotty's is a noted mining rendezvous. Small as it is, for a tavern, a large quantity of "cobblers," "streaks of lightning," and other drinks are here called for. Most of the up-country whiskey is well vitrioled, and almost makes one's throat raw. Here "a drink" costs from one to two shillings. Each person helps himself to as much as he pleases, without measure, but merely pouring into a tumbler from the spirit-bottle at the bar. There is a great deal of "standing treat" amongst the miners, and very expensive work it often proves, in more ways than one. A member of our party allowed himself to be persuaded into accepting two such gratuitous proffers from a miner who entered the tavern with fifty-two dollars of hard-earned money, all of which he spent in drinking here, and treating the company present. Our friend was rendered unfit for travel for days, through the two draughts of the mixture. It completely upset him; and much rest, fresh air, and exercise were found needful to restore him to his previous vigorous health. Whilst staying here we were very crowded, as the small building was filled with miners by day and night, sleeping under the table and benches as well as on top of them, and all over the floor. Miners, in these parts and elsewhere, become so accustomed to their rough way of life, as to prefer sleeping on a floor, or even on the bare ground, if only dry, rather than in a soft bed.

Drinking and gambling are the greatest bane of the miner. The former ruins his constitution rapidly, owing to the vile stuff with which the liquors here are sold are drugged. At the capital of British Columbia (New Westminster) a man is now under sentence of imprisonment for life, for a murder committed when overcome by the maddening influence of drink. He was, in general, a remarkably civil and quiet man, but on this occasion, having drunk too much whiskey, shot one of his comrades with scarcely any provocation, and, on coming to his sober consciousness, was astounded at what he had done, and at finding himself under arrest for a capital crime. It was expected that he would be hung; but the jury took a merciful view of the case, and brought in a verdict of manslaughter. This, however, involved chains and confinement for life—a terrible prospect for a vigorous and usually steady young man of thirty-five. It is sad but striking warning for his companions.

After leaving Scotty's we only proceeded four miles further down, when we reached McLean's Station, the best farm in the colony. The enterprising and industrious proprietor has valuable stock of cattle, especially some fine short-horns. Here we replenished our exhausted stock of flour at the comparatively low price of two shillings per pound. Fine turnips, cabbages, and scarlet-runners were growing hereabouts—a sight by no means common in British Columbia. This district, including Gavin's Creek, is a very good one for agriculture and for breeding cattle and horses. The water is excellent, and the climate very favorable.

THE LAKES - A HALT

OUR NEXT STAGE WAS TO another thriving farm - "The Lakes," so named from several picturesque sheets of water near it. The owner of the estate was urgently in need of assistance in several ways, and made our small party of three an offer for our services. As our funds were now all but totally exhausted, we gladly fell in with the proposal, and remained here three months, rendering assistance in various departments of labour. Thus, we first cut some reed and thatched the hay-stacks (a practice not usual in America); then we felled some trees, and erected a smith's shop and forge. Our stay here was mutually pleasant, and all the time the weather was beautifully clear— scarcely even a cloud across the bright blue expanse of the heavens. That quiet autumn in British Columbia will be long remembered by us, especially from its contrast with the previous two months of weary toil, disappointment, and hard- ships.

On the approach of winter we deemed it time to secure our retreat to the coast, took leave of our friends at "The

Lakes," and resumed the changing scenes of pedestrian travel. Our first night out was spent on a narrow rocky ledge on the steep declivity of a mountain overhanging the Thompson River, which flowed more than a thousand feet beneath us; and, as the darkness had overtaken us whilst mid-way in this dangerous pass, we were necessitated to remain in this most uncomfortable position till day-break. We may here remark that there is but little twilight in British Columbia. Night succeeds the day more rapidly than at home. Thus we found it to our cost on this occasion. A more miserable night we never spent; cramped in our lofty post of danger, the rain beating heavily upon us, drenched and shivering, yet afraid to stir, our thoughts turned with lively interest to memories of our English comfort, before we had been thus beguiled into crossing ocean and mountain, for the unattainable treasures of this vaunted El Dorado of the West. At five o'clock in the morning we gladly moved forwards, and soon reached the ferry across the Thompson, ten miles from "The Lakes."

The means here adopted for crossing is only suitable for streams where there is a strong current; but with such it succeeds very well, as on the Trent, between Nottingham and Wilford. A strong cable is stretched permanently across the river. With this the flat ferryboat is connected by two ropes running in blocks, from each end of the latter, to a single block sliding along the main cable. By keeping the boat in a diagonal position athwart the stream, the strength of the current impels the former along, as the blocks are successively shifted by a pull from the helmsman.

The ferry is the starting-point for the well-known dépot of the Hudson's Bay Company at Fort Kamloops or Thompson, sixty miles eastward, to which place a trail starts hence across the mountains. Our route, however, was still southward, down the river. Twelve miles farther brought us to Nicomin. From this point a good waggon-road extends to Yale.

On our way hither from the ferry we witnessed a curious spectacle. Some men were engaged in blasting the rocks beneath a tremendous precipice, for a continuation of the new waggon route on level ground, instead of the present trail over the lofty mountain, two thousand feet above them. Whilst we were watching the work awhile, we heard a rushing noise, and, looking up saw a large body coming down headlong from the elevated trail. It proved to be a splendid mule, which had made a false step and so fallen headlong. Of course the poor beast was killed instantaneously. A small encampment of Indians near by immediately came hastening in to secure the tempting prize as a feast. Men and women, with papooses, all clustered around the carcass, which they speedily cut up and carried off in pieces. Their delight found expression in loud cries of "Muck-muck," *i. e.*, something good to eat. They cook the flesh by holding it on a stick over a fire, warm the outside a little, and then greedily devour and gnaw it, as dogs with a bone.

The blasting party engaged here consisted of twentyfive or thirty miners, all of whom had been to Cariboo, but had returned down country, disappointed. Yet so thoroughly convinced were they of the existence of a large quantity of the precious metal at the diggings, that all were resolved to try their success once more next spring. They declared "the gold is there, sure enough; and we're bound to have some of it before we go home." Several of them had already secured claims at the mines, which they worked on till the rain and frost compelled their abandonment for the season; but they looked forward with confidence to the resumption of operations there. We heartily wished them success, for they were a fine lot of men, true Britons to the core, bold as lions, and almost as hardy and weather-proof as the rocks they were now quarrying.

LYTTON

Twelve miles below Nicomin is Lytton, named after Sir E. B. Lytton Bulwer, when sometime Secretary for the Colonies. It is situated at the point where the Thompson unites with the Fraser. Here we received a kind invitation to spend the night in front of a blazing fire in a strong iron store. After our usual devoirs to the "weed," we especially enjoyed our warm stretch-out in such comfortable quarters, so secure from wind, rain, and cold; for winter was now fairly commencing.

The Indians here, who were daily expecting the snow, had completed their winter huts. We descended into one of these, and may describe their nature. A circular hole is first excavated in the ground to the depth of seven feet, and having a diameter of twenty feet. This forms the body of the dwelling, or temporary cellar. The top is covered with a conical roof, elevated three feet above the surface of the ground, and having a hole in its center for egress and entrence, and for the outlet of smoke. A tree notched at the side (resembling the bear-pole in the Regent's Park Zoological Gardens) serves alike for the central prop of the roof and for the staircase of admission to the subterranean premises. A fire is lighted on the ground, immediately under the central hole at the top. Men, women, and children (the latter perfectly destitute of clothing) are here huddled together as each hut is inhabited by three or four families. We descended, and met with a civil, though grave reception on our being announced as "King George men." We were glad to re-emerge into the cold, but fresh, pure atmosphere above, as the foul air of these oven-like dens is most oppressive to a stranger. Whilst thus hibernating, the Indians subsist on dried fish, berries, and roots, and often on all three together, formed into a heterogeneous compound or soup. The roofs of these abodes are formed of strong logs thickly intertwined with brushwood, which, being well slanted and covered with earth, become almost impervious to rain and snow. The opening at the top is nearly closed; thus their condition is most unfavourable to health, and, as a consequence, many of them die of diseases thus contracted or aggravated. Last season was a very fatal one to them: numbers were swept away by the small-pox. When once seized with this malady they scarcely ever recover.

When staying at "The Lakes," we had seen a spot where about twelve wretched Indians had been buried by some of the settlers in the neighbourhood. All had been seized with small-pox, and, immediately on the appearance of the disease amongst them, their fellow-countrymen had abandoned them to their inevitable fate. The dread of disease by the Indians far surpasses their fear of violent or sudden death. The manner in which the sick and dying are thus forsaken by their companions is merely one amongst numerous illustrations of the degradation and depravity of human nature when not enlightened by the blessed influence of the Gospel, prompting at self-risk to seek the good of others. A beautiful contrast is afforded by the abundant instances where pestilence and death have been fearlessly braved even by tender and delicate Christian women, under the beneficent impulses of their holy religion. In case of the abandoned Indians just referred to, they all died one after another, and remained unburied for days, until their bodies attracted the attention of some white neighbours, who, by means of long poles and rakes, managed to thrust the remains of the poor wretches into one common grave, dug for them hard by the scene of their desolate death.

The miners' vice of gambling has been adopted by the poor Indians, who have learnt, in a manner of their own, to play at cards. Horses, blankets, and even their last garment are staked on the game. We have met them thus literally stripped, after their losses in this way amongst themselves.

FORT YALE AND THE COAST

For the remainder of our journey coastward we were able to dispense with the use of a tent, as we found houses tolerably frequent along the line of route; and it was a double advantage to be thus sheltered at night, instead of in a leaky and frail tent, and also to be lightened of the burden of carrying the latter, which we now bestowed as a present upon some of our Indian acquaintances. The roads here were also a vast improvement upon the trails further inland; so that in less than three days from Lytton we reached Fort Yale, where we entirely divested ourselves of our packs, the heavy burdens which we had borne up and down the land for eight hundred miles.

Yale is a thriving town, likely to become an important emporium for up-country traffic. One of the wealthiest men and principal owners of the land in the place was a rough but honest Yankee collier, popularly known as "Old York." He left the coal-mines in the States some years ago for those in

Vancouver's Columbia, emigrated hither, and, shrewdly judging that Yale must necessarily, from its position, become a prosperous state, opened a store here, and invested all his earnings in the purchase of land in the most likely positions. His clever anticipations are rapidly being realized, and his fortune is already secured. Yet he continues to wear the same style of dress as when a poor collier—still the open-necked buttonless blue shirt without cuffs, the thick boots, bare head, and tight moleskin pants, reaching far short of the ankles. It may be safely presumed that his descendants will be less anxious to manifest in so unmistakable a manner the lowly origin of their fortunes.

Having now reached the navigable portion of Frazer's River again, we embarked on the steamer "Reliance" on the 15th of December, for New Westminster, and, after a run of ten hours, reached it the same evening. Here we observed that little alteration had taken place since our former visit. Next day we re-embarked on another steamer for Vancouver's Island, and reached Victoria the same night. The latter place had undergone considerable and rapid changes during the past half-year. A whole street had sprung up, and also many large buildings. We were pleased to find that Christmas festivities were not forgotten, but were busily being prepared for, as was indicated by the evergreen decorations and festoons in various parts of the town.

W. CHAMPNESS

CONCLUDING GENERAL OBSERVATIONS ON THE COLONY

Before concluding our reminiscences of British Columbia, we will make a few general observations, and in particular respecting the class of emigrants most likely to succeed there.

Of all our colonies there is none where physical strength, patience, and good temper are more essentially indispensable than here. It is utterly useless for persons of weak constitution, or feeble powers of endurance, to attempt the expedition to the up-country mines of Cariboo and the Creeks. Again, we would strongly dissuade any of our city friends from emigrating hither. Men accustomed to agriculture and other hard manual labour, to mining and quarrying, and to ordinary skilled mechanical labour—such, and such only, are the class, in general, whom we would invite to British Columbia for the present. The high prices of provisions and stores have already seen their maximum, and will probably steadily decrease as the roads become more developed, the traffic directed into regular channels, and the agricultural resources of the country rendered more available. . .

The development of good roads is being carried on with the most laudable energy and promptitude by the Colonial Government, and, whilst laying a firm basis for the increased prosperity of the country, is affording most valuable and timely employment to numbers of emigrants who have been unable to reach the mines, or have been disappointed on their arrival there. These facilities of transit will obviate the excessively arduous, expensive, and hazardous trails over lofty mountains and along terrific precipices.

We would not recommend intending emigrants to burden themselves with a large and expensive outfit for their land journey to Cariboo. Considering that much, if not all, of what they take may have to be carried on their own shoulders, for at least a portion of the way, they will do well to restrict their wardrobe to the following articles, in addition to the suit of clothes they have in wear:—viz., one pair of thick blankets; two woolen shirts; two pairs of worsted stockings; one stout pair of pants ("Bedford cord" is recommended); and, in particular, strong high-laced-up shoes of well-seasoned leather, and with wide heels. No tent should be brought from England, and no mining tools, as they will be obtained on reasonable terms in the colony, and even at the upper mines.

Very many emigrants attribute their want of success to their having come out with a too small supply of money, wholly inadequate to their expenses up to the mines, or to their maintenance and perseverance there until able to reach the gold. Considering the many numerous and inevitable expenses to be incurred, two hundred pounds may be mentioned as being almost the lowest sum of money to bear the new comer with

W. CHAMPNESS

settled basis of operations, still further westward, to the shores of China, Japan, and Asiatic Russia—thus uniting the utmost west and farthest east in one comprehensive union of enlightened intercourse and prosperity, both temporal and spiritual.

INDEX

Acapulco 30
accidents to pack animals 54,
    69, 70, 90
Alexander, Fort 46
Anderson Lake 46, 48
Anderson River 46
Antler 73
Antler Creek 8, 10, 68, 72
arrastra, Spanish 20
Aspinwall 8, 23
autumn in British Columbia 88
Axe Lake 53, 80

Baker, Mount 45
Barkerville 10
Baynes, Admiral 44
beaver 79
Beaver Lake 65, 74, 75, 76
Berens, Fort
Billy Barker 10
blasting party 91
Bold Mountain 10
Boston men 80
Bowes, Gordon E., portait 5
Bowes, Gordon E. 11, 13, 14, 15
Brammall, Patricia 16
Bridge Creek 75, 79, 81
Brigade route
British Columbia 7, 9, 10, 13,
    23, 42, 54
British Columbia, agriculture
    65. 66
British Columbia, climate of
    98, 99
British Columbia, concluding
    observations 96

British Columbia Historical
    Association 13

cacao 26
California 37, 38, 41
camel pack train 66
candles 72
Cariboo 7; 9, 10, 19, 51, 70, 72
Cariboo diggings 46
Cariboo Lake 47, 71
"Cariboo Restaurant" 48
Carnarvon (town) 46
Cascade range 46
cattle 86
Champness, W. 7, 8, 13, 15, 16
Chinese Joss-house 32
Chinese miners 51
Chinese population 37
Christmas festivities 95
Clinton 9
'clootchmen' 80
Colonel Moody (steamer) 47
Colonial Government 96, 97
"Colonial Hotel" 42
"Columbia House" 48
Columetza 60
Contra Costa 34
counterfeit coin 48, 49
cradle 18
Cunningham's (claim) 72

"Dashaways" 33
Davis' (claim) 72
Deep Creek 61
diggings 72
diving for coins 30

INDEX

double-barrel 83
Douglas, Governor 44
Douglas pine 66
Douglas road 9
Douglas (town) 47, 48
drinking and gambling 86

emigrants, German and Irish
    28, 29
emigrants, qualities needed 96
Esquimault 42, 43
expenses for emigrants 97, 98

Fairfield, Washington 15, 16
fallen trees 62
farming land 65
farmstead in British Columbia 77
Farraleones 31
ferryboat 89, 90
flumes 71
food 84
Fort Alexander 60
Fort Kamloops 90
Fort Yale 94
Fraser, Donald 7
Fraser river 7, 9, 45, 46, 91
freight rates 40

game 83
goal at Douglas (drawing) 45
Gavin's Creek 87
general stores 68
gold 72
gold mining 73
gold pan 17

Golden Gate 41
Golden Gate (drawing) 27
Golledge Lake 51
good wash 50
'government building' 49
Great Britain 44
Green Lake 53, 80, 83
Gulf of Georgia 45

Harrison Lake 8, 46, 47
Harrison River 46
Hope 46
Hornby, Captain 44
Hot Springs 46, 49
hotels, San Francisco 32
huts and stores 69

Indian burial ground 58
Indian relics 58, 59
Indian tree burial 58, 59
Indian winter hut 92
Indians 92
Indians, death of 93, 94
Indians, food of 92
Indians, gambling 94
Indians, head flattening 58
Indians of British Columbia
    9, 57, 58
Isthmus 28

Keithleys 74
Keithley's Creek 71
killed by a bear 64
King George men 80, 92
Kootanie mines 99

INDEX

ladies of Spanish extraction 35
Lake House 72
Last Chance 72
Leisure Hour, The 7
Lightning Canyon 72
Lilooett 8, 50
Lilooett Lake 46, 48
Little Lake 66
log bridge 62
log shanties 71
Long Tom 19
Loon Lake 53, 57, 80, 84
lost on a new trail 74, 76
Lytton 9, 46, 53, 91, 94

Macdonald, Mr. Duncan G. F. 57
McLean's Station 86
meadow land 78
meerschaum 84
milk and coffee 79
miners sleeping outdoors 81
  67, 71, 81
miners, starving 70, 71
miners, wages 73
mines, conditions in 73
miners, returning 60, 61, 62, 63,
mining law 98
Morice, Adrian Gabriel 15
mosquitoes 57, 75, 78, 80
mountain roads 55
muck-muck 90
mud 67
mud and swamp 62, 63
mule train catastrophe 68, 69
murder 33, 86

natives of British Columbia 80
New Westminster 8, 43, 45, 46, 95

'Old York' 94, 95
Orizaba (steamer) 28, 32
otter 79
outfit for miners 97

Pacific Ocean 25, 29
pack horses 53, 60
packing 52, 54, 56
packing food supplies 52
Panama 24, 26, 28
Panama huts (drawing) 25
Panama railway 24
Peterson's (claim) 72
plantain 26
porpoises 31
post office, San Francisco 41
printing 15
prospecting pan 82
provisions 71, 82

Quesnelle, Forks of 66, 67, 68
Quesnelle Lake 47
Quesnelle (river) 46

rattlesnake 84
Ravenswood 33
Reliance (steamer) 95
revolver, accidents 65
revolvers 83
river gorges 54
rocker 18
Rocky Mountains 45
Russian Hill 34

INDEX

Sacramento River 41
salmon 58
Sampson, William R. 11, 16
San Francisco 31, 32, 33, 34, 35,
    39, 40, 41, 42
San Francisco cabs 39
San Francisco markets 38
San Joaquin River 41
San Juan Island 44
scenery of British Columbia 56
Scotty's Ranch 80, 82
Secession war (Civil War) 36
'service berry' 77
Seton Lake 46
Sierra Nevada (steamer) 8, 42
sluice box 19
smallpox 93
Southampton 23
Spanish arrastra 20
Spring Valley 75, 78, 79
'square meal' 50, 60
St. Thomas 23
Stephens, John L. 24
Strait of Juan de Fuca 43
stream crossing 51, 53

Taylor, Bayard 37
Telegraph Hill 32

thatching haystacks 83
The Lakes 88, 89, 93
Thompson River 8, 9, 80, 81,
    89, 91
tree stumps, drawing out with
    cattle 47
trout 83
twenty dollar gold pieces 36
twilight

Vancouver's Island 43
Vanderbilt 28
vermin 57
Victoria 7, 8, 42, 43, 95
Vigilance Committee 34

Wellington boots 56
Wells, Fargo & Co. 40
wild animals 79
whiskey 85
wild fowl 82, 83
William S. 64
William's Creek 10, 72
William's Lake 53, 57, 60, 61, 75
wooden house 84

Yale, 9, 46, 90
Yandle, Philip A. 14, 16
Ye Galleon Press 11

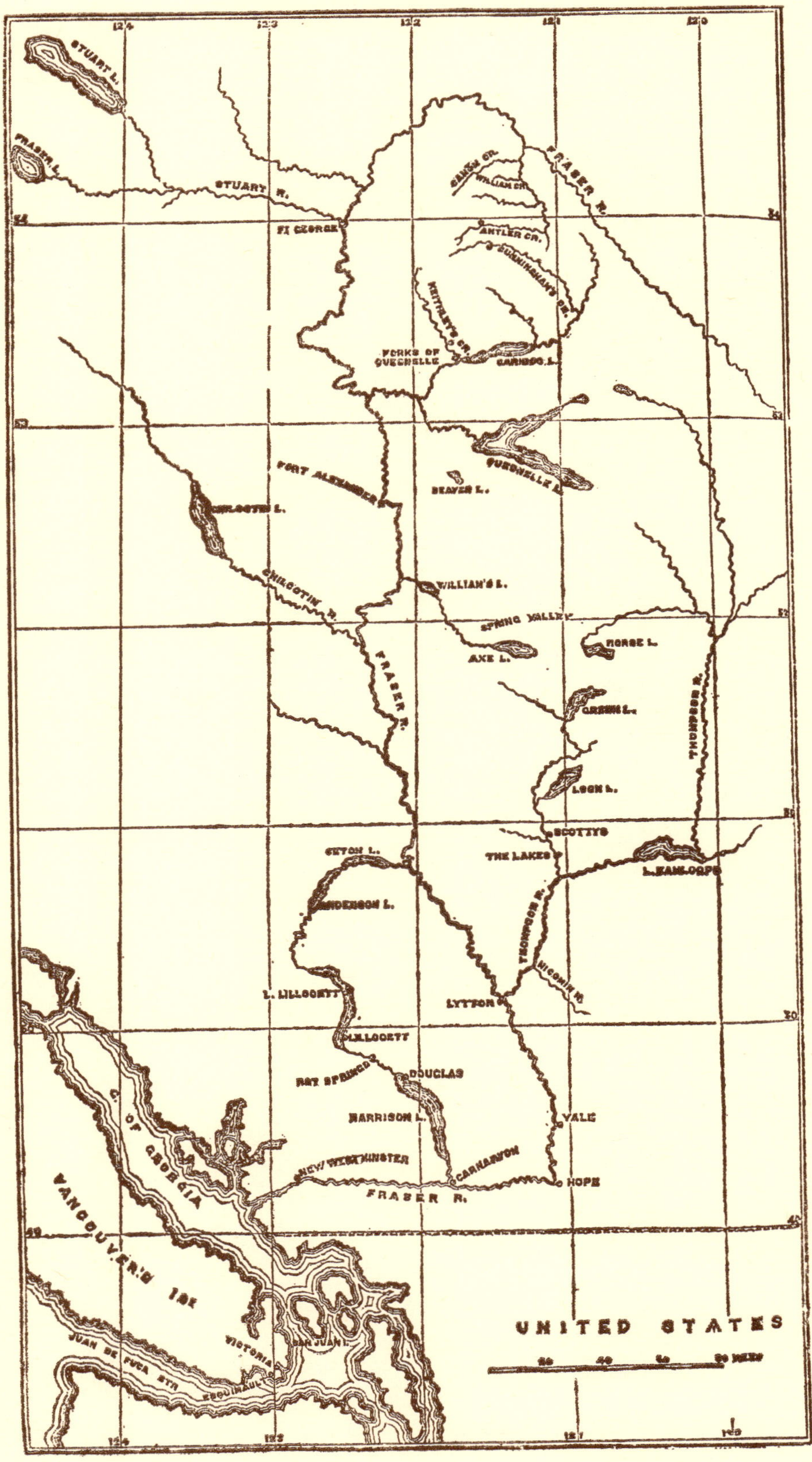

This is the Champness
map of British Columbia
and the Cariboo mining
district as printed in
London in 1865.

COLOPHON

The Champness text pages are set in fourteen point Baskerville with six points of leading between the lines. The text setting was by Don Rasmussen of Moses Lake, Washington. The designing and other typesetting was by Glen Adams. The title page is set in eighteen and twenty-four point Bembo with the word *Cariboo* in thirty-six point Diamond Inlaid. Artwork for the hand drawn printed end papers is by Robert Bluhm of Ephrata, Washington. Pen and ink drawings of the cradle, sluice box and Spanish arrastra are by Sister Mary Luke of Santa Cruz, California. The binding was done by William Bosch, Arts and Crafts, Spokane, Washington. The old Champness line drawings and the Bluhm end sheets were printed by Don Rasmussen on a 1936 Model LSB Harris offset press. All other printing was letterpress on a Vandercook Universal III proof press. The paper stock is sixty-five pound ivory Andorra cover.